LOUISI PLANTATION HOMES POSTCARD BOOK

Photography by Paul Malone
Text by Lee Malone

PELICAN PUBLISHING COMPANY
Gretna 1999

*The word "Pelican" and the depiction of a pelican are trademarks of
Pelican Publishing Company, Inc., and are registered
in the U.S. Patent and Trademark Office.*

ISBN: 1-56554-641-5

Printed in Hong Kong

Published by Pelican Publishing Company, Inc.
1000 Burmaster Street, Gretna, Louisiana 70053

Ardoyne, near Houma, Louisiana

PHOTO BY PAUL MALONE © LEE MALONE
LOUISIANA PLANTATION HOMES PUBLISHED BY PELICAN PUBLISHING COMPANY

To:

Place
Postage
Stamp
Here

Belle Oak, Marksville, Louisiana

To:

Catalpa, near St. Francisville, Louisiana

PHOTO BY PAUL MALONE © LEE MALONE
LOUISIANA PLANTATION HOMES PUBLISHED BY PELICAN PUBLISHING COMPANY

To:

Place
Postage
Stamp
Here

Destrehan, near New Orleans,
Louisiana

To:

Live Oaks, Rosedale,
Louisiana

To:

Glencoe, near Jackson,
Louisiana

To:

Grevemberg House, near
Franklin, Louisiana

PHOTO BY PAUL MALONE © LEE MALONE
LOUISIANA PLANTATION HOMES PUBLISHED BY PELICAN PUBLISHING COMPANY

To:

Dining room at L'Hermitage,
near Darrow, Louisiana

To:

Houmas House, near Burnside,
Louisiana

PHOTO BY PAUL MALONE © LEE MALONE
LOUISIANA PLANTATION HOMES PUBLISHED BY PELICAN PUBLISHING COMPANY

To:

Joseph Jefferson House, near
New Iberia, Louisiana

To:

Place
Postage
Stamp
Here

Layton Castle, Monroe,
Louisiana

To:

*Madewood, near Napoleonville,
Louisiana*

To:

Magnolia Lane, Westwego,
Louisiana

To:

African House at Melrose, near
Natchitoches, Louisiana

To:

The Myrtles, St. Francisville, Louisiana

PHOTO BY PAUL MALONE © LEE MALONE
LOUISIANA PLANTATION HOMES PUBLISHED BY PELICAN PUBLISHING COMPANY

To:

Nottoway, White Castle,
Louisiana

To:

Oak Alley, near Vacherie, Louisiana

To:

Oaklawn Manor, near Franklin,
Louisiana

To:

The Cottage, St. Francisville,
Louisiana

To:

Pitot House, New Orleans, Louisiana

To:

Place
Postage
Stamp
Here

Dining room at Propinquity,
St. Francisville, Louisiana

To:

Michel Prudhomme Home,
Opelousas, Louisiana

PHOTO BY PAUL MALONE © LEE MALONE
LOUISIANA PLANTATION HOMES PUBLISHED BY PELICAN PUBLISHING COMPANY

To:

L'Hermitage, near Darrow,
Louisiana

To:

Rosedown, St. Francisville,
Louisiana

PHOTO BY PAUL MALONE © LEE MALONE
LOUISIANA PLANTATION HOMES PUBLISHED BY PELICAN PUBLISHING COMPANY

To:

St. Louis Plantation House, near
Plaquemine, Louisiana

PHOTO BY PAUL MALONE © LEE MALONE
LOUISIANA PLANTATION HOMES PUBLISHED BY PELICAN PUBLISHING COMPANY

To:

San Francisco, Garyville,
Louisiana

To:

Place
Postage
Stamp
Here

Sauvinet-Lewis House,
New Orleans, Louisiana

To:

*Shadows-on-the-Teche, near
New Iberia, Louisiana*

PHOTO BY PAUL MALONE © LEE MALONE
LOUISIANA PLANTATION HOMES PUBLISHED BY PELICAN PUBLISHING COMPANY

To:

Steamboat House, New Orleans, Louisiana

To: